Explaining the 30-year shift in consumer expenditures from commodities to services, 1982–2012

Over the last 30 years, consumer expenditures in the United States have shifted from commodities to services. This article uses Consumer Price Index (CPI) and Consumer Expenditure Survey (CE) data to examine the key drivers of that shift. CPI and CE data show that the compositional change in consumer expenditures has been driven by a considerable increase in the quantity of owner-occupied shelter.

The last 30 years have seen a shift in the allocation of U.S. consumer expenditures from commodities to services. This article uses Consumer Expenditure Survey (CE) data and Consumer Price Index (CPI) "relative importance" and index data (1) to show that the shift has been driven by changes not only in price but also in quantity[1] and (2) to identify the particular categories of services driving the overall shift to services consumption. Focusing on *absolute* changes in per-household expenditures during the period 1984–2011, the article finds a 9.1-percent increase in the quantity of services and no change in the quantity of commodities. This trend has been driven largely by a considerable increase in owner-occupied shelter. The article also finds that the quantity of health care services has decreased, although the share of personal consumption expenditures (PCE) accounted for by health care services, as measured from 1959 to 2009 by the U.S. Bureau of Economic Analysis (BEA), has increased. This difference illustrates that PCE data account for third-party expenditures, while CPI and CE data do not.[2] Within commodities, the quantity of durable goods has increased, while the quantity of nondurables has decreased.

Focusing on *relative* changes in total expenditures for the 30-year period from December 1982 to December 2012, the analysis yields the same general result. There has been an increase in the total quantity of services at the expense of commodities—a shift primarily due to an increase in the quantity of shelter, in particular owner-occupied shelter. There has also been a considerable increase in the quantity of "other services" (a residual category not including shelter, transportation services, medical care services, and energy services), when "other services" are compared with commodities. Moreover, the decrease in the quantity of medical care services does not mean that consumers have consumed less medical care services; rather, it means that third-party expenditures have increased while out-of-pocket expenditures have decreased.

In short, CPI and CE data show that the shift to a services-based economy entails more shelter, while PCE data indicate that the shift is also driven by increases in expenditures on health care services. Within commodities, there has been an increase in the quantity of durables and a decrease in the quantity of nondurables.

Background

In 1968, economist Victor Fuchs observed that more than half of the employed population in the United States was working in the services sector and thus was "not involved in the production of food, clothing, houses, automobiles, or other tangible goods."[3] The U.S. economy, he argued, had become a "service economy."

Fuchs's analysis identified a fundamental change on the production side of the U.S. economy, a change in which the services sector had captured an increasing share of overall employment in the

United States. But a similar shift was also occurring on the consumption side of the U.S. economy, with consumers allocating an increasing share of total expenditures to services and a decreasing share to commodities. This change was already underway at the time of Fuchs's writing, and since then, the U.S. economy has not looked back.[4]

Detailed CE data show that, from 1984 to 2011, per-household nominal average annual expenditures on commodities increased from $10,292 to $18,408, an increase of 78.9 percent, and per-household nominal average annual expenditures on services increased from $9,643 to $26,732, an increase of 177.2 percent. These changes are part of a longer term trend in relative expenditures that has seen the share of total expenditures allocated to commodities decrease and the share allocated to services increase. For example, in the period 1947–1949, commodities made up 72.9 percent of total consumer expenditures, compared with 27.1 percent for services, as measured by historical CPI relative importance tables, which use CE data to compute the percent allocation of consumer expenditures across multiple categories of commodities and services. By 1968, these shares had changed to 64.2 percent and 35.8 percent, respectively. In 2012, the shares had reversed: consumer expenditures on commodities had dropped to 39.7 percent of total expenditures, with services accounting for the remaining 60.3 percent.[5] U.S. consumers now spend more money on services than on commodities. (See table 1.)

Table 1. Relative importance of CPI-U indexes for commodities and services, 1947–1949 to 2012 (in percent of all items)

Year	Commodities	Services
1947–1949	72.9	27.1
1960	63.7	36.3
1968	64.2	35.8
1970	62.9	37.2
1980	58.4	41.6
1990	45.3	54.7
2000	41.8	58.2
2005	40.8	59.2
2010	40.0	60.0
2012	39.7	60.3

Source: U.S. Bureau of Labor Statistics, CPI relative importance tables, www.bls.gov/cpi.

PCE data, an alternative source of information on consumption patterns produced by the BEA, show a similar trend. One BEA analysis reveals that the "share of current-dollar PCE accounted for by services increased from 45.7 percent in 1959 to 67.7 percent in 2009."[6]

This fundamental change on the consumption side of the U.S. economy was driven, in part, by changes in relative price. As the prices of commodities rose at a lower rate than did the prices of services, the fraction of total consumer expenditures allocated to commodities decreased as well. Indeed, from 1968 to 2012, the CPI for All Urban Consumers (CPI-U) for commodities increased by 377.3 percent, which is equivalent to an average annual rate of change of 3.6 percent. Over the same period, the CPI-U for services increased by 780.0 percent, which is equivalent to an average annual rate of change of 5.1 percent. (See table 2.) PCE data show a similar trend. The BEA analysis referenced above reveals that, from 1959 to 2009, "services prices increased at an average rate of 4.4 percent, nearly 2 percentage points more than the 2.6 percent change in goods prices."[7]

Table 2. Cumulative and average annual rates of change in the CPI-U indexes for commodities and services, 1950–2012 (in percent)

| Period | Commodities[1] | | Services[1] | |
	Cumulative	Annual	Cumulative	Annual
1950–2012	509.20	3.00	1,482.00	4.60
1960–2012	446.30	3.30	1,026.30	4.80
1968–2012	377.30	3.60	780.00	5.10
1970–2012	335.80	3.60	656.10	4.90
1980–2012	106.70	2.30	233.80	3.80
1990–2012	47.00	1.80	92.30	3.00
2000–2012	23.50	1.80	38.20	2.70
2005–2012	15.80	2.10	17.40	2.30

Notes:

[1] Percent changes are calculated from December of the beginning year to December of the final year.
Source: U.S. Bureau of Labor Statistics, CPI data, www.bls.gov/cpi.

Even though consumers faced larger increases in the price of services, they nonetheless purchased a greater *quantity* of services. This article dissects the implicit price and quantity components of total dollar expenditures to show that the shift in expenditures was driven by changes not only in price but also in quantity. Moreover, commodities and services are disaggregated into major component categories (defined by CPI special aggregate indexes) to examine their expenditure, price, and quantity trends over the last quarter century, and to determine their relative influence on the overall shift from commodities to services. Because of the importance of the shelter index in the analysis, the article focuses on per-household expenditures during the period 1984–2011 and on total urban consumer expenditures from December 1982 to December 2012 and finds that the shift in quantity from commodities to services during both periods was driven largely by an increase in the quantity of shelter.[8] In addition, there has been a relative shift in quantity from commodities to "other services" (e.g., cable television and Internet services) and to energy services (natural gas and electricity). Finally, the composition of commodities consumption has seen a decrease in the quantity of nondurable goods (e.g., food and apparel) and an increase in the quantity of durable goods (e.g., appliances and televisions).

The sections below examine in greater detail the trends in price, quantity, and expenditures for commodities and services. The next section summarizes the CE and CPI survey design methodology to illustrate how the CE and the CPI can serve as sources of information on changes over time in consumer preferences for commodities and services available in the marketplace. The section that follows provides an overview, based on CE data, of changes in average annual expenditures on commodities and services and deflates these changes with the use of appropriate CPI indexes to present an overview of absolute changes in quantity. The analysis then compares commodities and services, and their major component aggregates, against each other to determine whether one has become relatively more (less) expensive than the other and whether any observed difference in price has resulted in relatively less (more) quantity of a category being consumed over the examined period.

Consumer preferences in the CE and the CPI

The CPI is a measure of the average change over time in the prices paid by urban consumers for a "market basket" of goods and services, that is, a sample of goods and services that consumers purchase for day-to-day living. Produced monthly by the Bureau of Labor Statistics (BLS), the CPI weights each item in the market basket on the basis of the amount of spending reported by a sample of families and individuals. Widely used as a measure of inflation, the CPI is based on data collected in surveys that also provide useful information on changes in relative demand among U.S. consumers.

Price indexes are designed to measure the change in expenditure necessary to purchase a constant-quality market basket of goods and services.[9] The CPI has two primary inputs: prices and expenditure weights. The prices are collected from two surveys: the Commodities and Services (C&S) Survey and the Housing Survey.[10] Expenditure weights, the second input to price indexes, are based on CE data collected by the U.S. Census Bureau for BLS.

The CE identifies the dollar amount people spend on a broad range of goods and services. About 14,000 1-week diaries and 28,000 quarterly interviews are collected from the current CE sample each year. Until 1980, the survey was conducted about every 10 years. Since then, it has been conducted on an ongoing basis, with tables published annually.

The CE data are used as the source of expenditure weights in CPI indexes, as well as the source of "relative importance" tables historically produced by BLS on an annual basis. These tables contain the percent allocation of expenditures across all categories of commodities and services purchased by urban U.S. consumers, and thus provide comprehensive information on the overall composition of U.S. consumption over time. Until January 2002, CE data were used to update CPI weights approximately every 10 years. The CPI switched to biennial updating in January 2002.

The relative importance tables make it possible to identify changes over time in consumer expenditure allocations across the broad range of commodity and service categories for which CPI indexes are calculated. For example, urban consumers in the United States allocated approximately 6.2 percent of total expenditures to food away from home (restaurant meals, vending machines, mobile food trucks, etc.) in 2001, compared with 5.7 percent in 2012. By contrast, urban consumers allocated 5.8 percent of total expenditures on medical care in 2001, compared with 7.2 percent in 2012.

Food away from home and medical care are specific categories of goods and services for which indexes and expenditure allocations are computed. These indexes fall within the traditional aggregation structure of the CPI, in which indexes are computed for 8 major expenditure categories, 70 expenditure classes, and 211 item strata.[11] In addition to the traditional aggregation structure, the CPI produces special aggregate indexes in which lower level indexes are grouped into special categories, such as "all items less food and energy" or "all items less medical care." Two special categories, which together encompass the full set of CPI indexes, are those for commodities and services.

There is not necessarily a one-to-one match between the specific goods and services tracked in the CE and the specific goods and services priced in the CPI. Expenditure weights are produced for all 211 basic item-area index cells (the lowest level of index construction), that is, for categories of goods and services, not for individual goods and services. Thus, inferences about shifts in consumer demand can be made only about categories of items, not about specific items. For example, inferences can be drawn that there has been a shift in quantity from commodities to services, or from nondurables to durables, but not that there has been a shift, say, from magazines to a specific package of cable television services.

In sum, data collected for use in the CPI can be used to measure shifting consumer preferences for various types of commodities and services currently available in the marketplace. In particular, the CE provides data on how dollar expenditures have shifted among various categories of commodities and services. BLS publishes annual relative importance tables that convert these dollar expenditures into a percent allocation of expenditures across the many categories of goods and services purchased by consumers.[12] CE and CPI expenditure data implicitly contain a price component and a quantity component. In the analysis below, these components are identified and analyzed to examine absolute and relative changes in consumption.

Toward a service economy: the rise of shelter

This section examines *absolute* changes in per-household expenditures on, and quantity of, commodities and services. It also considers changes in expenditure and quantity for the major component categories of commodities and services associated with CPI special aggregate indexes. These special aggregates are shelter, owners' equivalent rent, transportation services, medical care services, "other services," energy services, durables, and nondurables.

CE detailed expenditure data containing information on average annual expenditures per household at the most granular levels of disaggregation were obtained for the years 1984 and 2011. CE data are not categorized under commodities and services, or under CPI special aggregate groupings that can be assigned to either commodities or services, but instead are aligned with the traditional CPI aggregation structure and include categories such as food, housing, apparel, entertainment, transportation, medical care, personal care, and miscellaneous. These detailed groupings of data were thus manually assigned to special aggregate categories and summed to obtain expenditures for commodities and services and their major component aggregates. (See table A–1 in the appendix for a detailed listing of CE items mapped to each CPI special aggregate category.)

The resulting expenditures were analyzed to obtain percent changes in expenditures. CPI indexes were used to deflate percent changes in expenditures and then derive absolute percent changes in quantity.[13] These derivations can be obtained from basic calculations involving price and quantity. The percent change in absolute quantity is given by

$$[P_1 Q_1 / P_0 Q_0] / (P_1/P_0) = Q_1/Q_0,$$

where P_0 and Q_0 are price and quantity in 1984, and P_1 and Q_1 are price and quantity in 2011. The product P_0Q_0 represents expenditures in 1984, and P_1Q_1 represents expenditures in 2011. The calculation of absolute quantity is the equivalent of deflating changes in expenditures by the change in the price index for the particular special aggregate category of the CPI examined. For example, from 1984 to 2011, average annual expenditures on commodities increased by 78.9 percent. Dividing this change by the change in the index for commodities yields a 0.4-percent increase in per-household quantity of commodities purchased, meaning that the per-household quantity of commodities was essentially unchanged. A similar calculation for services, for which average annual expenditures increased by 177.2 percent over the study period, yields a 9.1-percent increase in quantity after accounting for price change. Table 3 summarizes the results of these calculations for commodities and services, as well as special aggregate groupings of commodities and services.

Table 3. Changes in price, quantity, and expenditures for categories of consumer spending defined by CPI special aggregate indexes, 1984–2011

Category	Average annual expenditures		Expenditure change (percent)	Price change (percent)	Quantity change (percent)
	1984	2011			
Commodities	$10,292	$18,408	78.85	78.16	0.39
Services	9,643	26,732	177.20	154.07	9.10
Shelter[1]	4,538	13,093	188.51	143.46	18.51
Services less shelter[2]	5,100	13,639	167.43	167.79	-0.13
Owners' equivalent rent (OER)	3,505	10,188	190.69	141.91	20.17
Services less OER	6,133	16,544	169.74	162.86	2.62
Other services	1,824	4,896	168.34	195.24	-9.11
Services less other services	7,814	21,836	179.47	148.62	12.41
Transportation services	1,051	2,539	141.69	155.73	-5.49
Services less transportation services	8,587	24,193	181.72	153.84	10.98
Health care services	825	2,692	226.44	297.20	-17.81
Services less health care services	8,813	24,040	172.77	142.87	12.31
Energy services	926	1,843	99.04	84.43	7.92
Services less energy services	8,712	24,889	185.68	161.30	9.33

Category	Average annual expenditures		Expenditure change (percent)	Price change (percent)	Quantity change (percent)
	1984	2011			
Durables	3,238	4,819	48.85	7.10	38.99
Nondurables	7,053	13,588	92.65	113.71	-9.85

Notes:

[1] Expenditures are deflated by the CPI for "rent of shelter."

[2] Expenditures are deflated by the CPI for "services less rent of shelter."

Note: CE detailed unpublished tables contain estimates of more detailed categories of spending that are subject to larger standard errors.

Source: CE detailed unpublished tables.

Table 3 contains the changes in expenditure, price, and quantity for aggregate categories, such as transportation services and medical care services.[14] Transportation services include such items as auto rentals, airline fares, and towing charges. Health care services include such items as physician services and hospital services. This study examines changes in out-of-pocket expenditures and quantity for aggregate categories, not for specific items within these aggregate categories. This distinction is important because the composition of the market basket (to which expenditures pertain) changed over the 1984–2011 period. Physician services in 1984 were different from physician services in 2011; so, an increase in "quantity" does not necessarily mean that consumers buy more of the same thing. Instead, the change in quantity is understood as a residual between changes in expenditures and changes in price and can be interpreted to mean that consumers buy "more" or "less" of a category of commodity or service, depending on whether the change in quantity is positive or negative. Consumers buy more or less of the same *type* of thing.

The components of services that show the most substantial increases in quantity are shelter and owners' equivalent rent (OER). The quantity of shelter and OER increased by 18.5 percent and 20.2 percent, respectively, while everything else in services (services less shelter, services less OER) remained essentially unchanged.[15] As explained in the next section, these increases are corroborated by increasing rates of homeownership and an increase in the median square footage of floor size of new single-family homes in the Unites States—an increase from 1,520 square feet in 1982 to 2,169 square feet in 2010.[16]

The quantity of "other services," which contain CE items mapped to the CPI special aggregate category "other services" (e.g., telephone and Internet services; tuition and child care; admission fees to sporting and entertainment events; cable television; personal care services; and miscellaneous expenses, such as funeral expenses, legal fees, and checking account fees), decreased by 9.1 percent.[17] Transportation services decreased by 5.5 percent. Energy services increased by 7.9 percent (as the purchase of shelter has increased, so has the purchase of natural gas and electricity).

Although the quantity of health care services decreased by 17.8 percent—a finding that may come as a surprise given an aging population and the growth of the health care industry—it is important to distinguish between total consumption expenditures and consumption attributed to consumers' out-of-pocket expenditures. It is indeed the case that total consumption expenditures on health care services have increased over the long term. As explained in the BEA study on long-term consumption referenced earlier, "among PCE services categories, the largest increases in shares were for health care services and for financial services and insurance. The share of PCE accounted for by health care services increased from 4.7 percent in 1959 to 16.2 percent in 2009, while the share accounted for by financial services and insurance increased from 3.9 percent in 1959 to 8.1 percent in 2009. . . . Together, these categories accounted for more than two-thirds of the increase in the services share of PCE."[18] This increase in consumption expenditures for health care services was driven by large increases in employer-provided health care, government expenditures on Medicare and Medicaid, an aging population, and substantial advances in medical care technology.[19]

The BEA analysis on PCE trends also explains that, "in 1959, 72.7 percent of PCE for health care was paid for by direct out-of-pocket expenditures, and by 2009, this share had declined to 17.6 percent. During this period, the share of PCE for health care paid for by government increased from 3.4 percent to 45.4 percent."[20] The health care marketplace in later years undoubtedly consists of much higher quality services that have benefitted consumers,[21] but consumers pay much less out of pocket for such services, a trend highlighting a "significant decrease in the share of PCE accounted for by out-of-pocket expenditures."[22]

The CPI for financial services includes only checking accounts and other bank services, as well as tax return preparation and other accounting fees, and has less than 0.5-percent share in the CPI.[23] The PCE, however, is a more expansive category, which includes such items as pension funds, regulated investment companies (such as mutual funds), and securities commissions. According to the BEA article, "the increased share of financial services was associated with greatly increased holdings of regulated investment company—also known as mutual fund—assets by households, greatly increased use of credit cards, and large increases in the fees of banks and other depository institutions."[24]

Within commodities, the quantity of durables (e.g., appliances, personal computers, new vehicles, sporting goods)[25] increased by 39.0 percent, while the quantity of nondurables (e.g., food, clothing, and medical care commodities)[26] decreased by 9.9 percent. This indicates that the shift from commodities to shelter has been accompanied by a decrease in the quantity of traditional nondurable necessities, such as food and clothing, as well as an increase in the quantity of appliances, personal computers, new vehicles, sporting goods, and other durable goods. The PCE data also show a shift toward durable goods. From 1959 to 2009, the quantity of durable goods consumed increased at an average annual rate of 5.2 percent, compared with 2.5 percent for nondurable goods. Moreover, "the share (of PCE) accounted for by food and beverages decreased by 11.6 percentage points, from 19.4 percent to 7.8 percent, and the share accounted for by clothing and footwear decreased by 4.8 percentage points, from 8.0 percent to 3.2 percent."[27]

Table 3 highlights that the increased quantity of durable goods is associated with a small increase in the price of durable goods and that this small increase contrasts with the considerable increase in the price of nondurable goods. Expenditures on nondurables are still almost three times as large as expenditures on durable goods. In the next section, CPI relative importance figures show that durable commodities comprised only 8.8 percent of total consumer expenditures in 2012, compared with 13.1 percent in 1982; nondurable commodities comprised 30.9 percent of expenditures in 2012, compared with 39.9 percent in 1982. Consumers still spend more on nondurable items, such as food and clothing, but nondurables have become relatively more expensive and the quantity of durables has increased in the overall market basket of goods and services.

It is easily observed, then, that a considerable increase in the quantity of shelter has driven the overall shift from commodities to services. This finding contrasts with the findings of the BEA study of PCE data, which suggest that health care and financial services have driven the shift from goods to services. This difference in findings reflects differences in the scope and weight of measurement in the

CPI and the PCE. The PCE weight on health care reflects third-party expenditures by employers and government, while the CPI does not.[28] The result is a higher weight on health care in the PCE than in the CPI, and a higher relative weight on shelter in the CPI than in the PCE. This difference in weight reflects the role of out-of-pocket expenditures in the CPI. Thus, the CPI measures consumption expenditures for which the cost is borne by consumers, whereas the PCE measures all consumption expenditures for the benefit of consumers.[29]

The upshot is that the shift in quantity from commodities to services in the CPI has been driven largely by an increase in the quantity of shelter. More households have chosen to own homes than to rent. Those which own homes have tended to buy bigger homes, driving up demand for natural gas and electricity, trash and garbage collection, home appliances, and other items. Meanwhile, as total consumption expenditures have increased, out-of-pocket expenditures on health care services have decreased. In short, CPI and CE data show that the average household in the United States consumed relatively more shelter, as well as more durable items, in 2011 than in 1984, while PCE data show that the consumption of health care and financial services has increased even as out-of-pocket expenditures have decreased.

Toward a service economy: changes in the composition of the CPI market basket

In the previous section, CE data were used to obtain *absolute* changes in per-household expenditure and quantity. Expenditures were decomposed into price and quantity components to determine the overall increase or decrease in quantity of a specific category of consumer expenditure. In this section, CPI relative importance tables, which are constructed from CE data, are used to obtain *relative* changes in expenditures and quantity. The purpose is to examine changes in the composition of the CPI market basket by comparing commodities and services, and their major component aggregates, against each other, to determine relative changes in price and quantity.

Methodology. CPI relative importance data can be used to obtain the relative expenditure for a CPI category, such as commodities, at a specific point in time. Relative importance data for particular categories of expenditures are published as percentages of total expenditures, so that "all items" has a weight of 100 (i.e., 100 percent of total expenditures are spent on all items). These percentages can be interpreted as relative dollar expenditures, where a weight of 100 percent can be interpreted as $100 spent on all items. Thus, the relative importance of a CPI category in a "base" year can be interpreted as a scaled, or normalized, expenditure equal to $P_0 Q_0$. The relative importance, or expenditure, in a later year is $P_1 Q_1$.

These relative importances, or expenditures, can be divided into a price component and a quantity component. Holding quantity constant, the change in total expenditure resulting only from a change in price can be obtained. Similarly, holding price constant, the expenditure resulting only from a change in quantity can be obtained. Using these calculations, the implicit price and quantity components of a change in relative expenditure (i.e., relative importance) can be obtained, thereby isolating the real change in consumption (i.e., change in the quantity composition of the market basket) over time.

To obtain the expenditure based purely on price change, $P_0 Q_0$ can be multiplied by the change in the index P_1/P_0 to obtain $P_1 Q_0$. $P_1 Q_0$ can be calculated for any two or more expenditure categories, such as commodities and services. The relative change in quantity for each category can then be obtained by dividing the expenditure in the later year ($P_1 Q_1$) by the expenditure based on the pure price effect ($P_1 Q_0$), where expenditures based on pure price change ($P_1 Q_0$) are normalized so that shares sum to

100, and thus expenditures continue to be interpreted as shares of $100 spent on everything. Table 4 provides an example of these calculations for the relative shift from commodities to services.

Table 4. Example of relative price and quantity calculations, commodities vs. services, December 1982– December 2012

Period	Definition	Commodities	Services	Calculation
%ΔP Dec 1982–Dec 2012 (absolute percent change)	(a)	88.20	183.00	$((P_1/P_0) - 1)*100$
December 1982 weight	(b)	52.908	47.092	P_0Q_0
December 2012 weight	(c)	39.680	60.320	P_1Q_1
December 2012 weight if $Q_1 = Q_0$	(d) = ((b)*(1 + (a)/100))	99.573	133.270	$P_1Q_0 = (P_0Q_0)*(P_1/P_0)$
December 2012 weight if $Q_1 = Q_0$ (normalized)	(e)	42.764	57.236	$P_1Q_0 = (P_0Q_0)*(P_1/P_0)$
%ΔQ Dec 1982–Dec 2012 (relative percent change)	(f) = ((c)/(e) – 1)*100	-7.21	5.39	$\%\Delta Q = ((P_1Q_1/P_1Q_0) - 1)*100$
%ΔP Dec 1982–Dec 2012 (relative percent change)	(g) = ((e)/(b) – 1)*100	-19.17	21.54	$\%\Delta P=((P_1Q_0/P_0Q_0) - 1)*100$

Note: P_0 and Q_0 represent price and quantity in 1982, and P_1 and Q_1 represent price and quantity in 2012.
Source: U.S. Bureau of Labor Statistics and author's calculations.

For the CPI-U (urban) population, the share of total consumer expenditures attributed to commodities decreased from 52.9 percent in December 1982 to 40.0 percent in December 2012, while the share attributed to services increased from 47.1 percent to 60.3 percent over the same period. Based on the calculations described in the previous paragraph, it can be shown that if the quantity of commodities consumed was unchanged, so that any change in expenditures was caused only by a change in price, the share of consumer expenditures spent on commodities would have decreased to 42.8 percent, while the share spent on services would have increased to 57.2 percent (after normalization). This calculation indicates that the *relative* price (as opposed to the absolute change in price) of commodities decreased, while the *relative* price of services increased. In other words, in December 2012, consumers were able to buy more units of commodities per unit of services given up than they were in December 1982. Alternatively, in December 2012, consumers were able to buy fewer units of services per unit of commodities given up.

Based on this methodology, the change in relative quantity can be calculated as the percent difference between the normalized expenditure weights that would have prevailed under a pure price change and the actual expenditure weights from the CPI relative importance tables. Despite the decline in the relative price of commodities, the relative quantity of commodities turns out to have decreased by 7.2 percent, while the relative quantity of services has increased by 5.4 percent. This relative change in quantity was associated with a relative price decrease of 19.2 percent for commodities and a relative price increase of 21.5 percent for services. Although services have become relatively more expensive, the market basket contains relatively more services and relatively fewer commodities today than it did in December 1982.

The relative shift from commodities to services within the overall consumption basket purchased by consumers is unmistakable. But the commodities and services indexes are comprised of a large and diverse set of indexes, or commodity and service categories, such as food, apparel, energy commodities, rent of primary residence, owners' equivalent rent of residences, transportation services, medical care services, energy services, and "other services." Each of these indexes contributes to the all-items CPI, and, as such, attracts a certain percentage of the overall allocation of total expenditures by urban consumers. This percentage is the relative importance of the index. The following discussion explores which categories of services have driven the overall reallocation of expenditures and quantity from commodities to services.

Overview of changes in the relative importance of commodity and service categories. Figures 1 and 2 present the relative importance of major categories of commodities and services. The figures generally show that the expenditure shares of commodity indexes are decreasing, while the expenditure shares of services indexes are increasing. In figure 1, it can be observed that the relative importances of both durable and nondurable commodities decrease over the study period. The relative importances of consumer necessities such as food and apparel also decrease (the trend is harder to see for apparel, but apparel's relative importance declined from 4.4 percent to 3.6 percent over the period).[30] "Core" commodities (i.e., "commodities less energy commodities") and energy commodities both decreased in relative importance, although energy commodities were more volatile. The importance of groceries (food at home) declined from 12.9 percent to 8.6 percent, while that of food away from home declined from 6.1 percent to 5.7 percent.

Figure 1. Relative importance of specific CPI-U commodity indexes, December 1982–December 2012

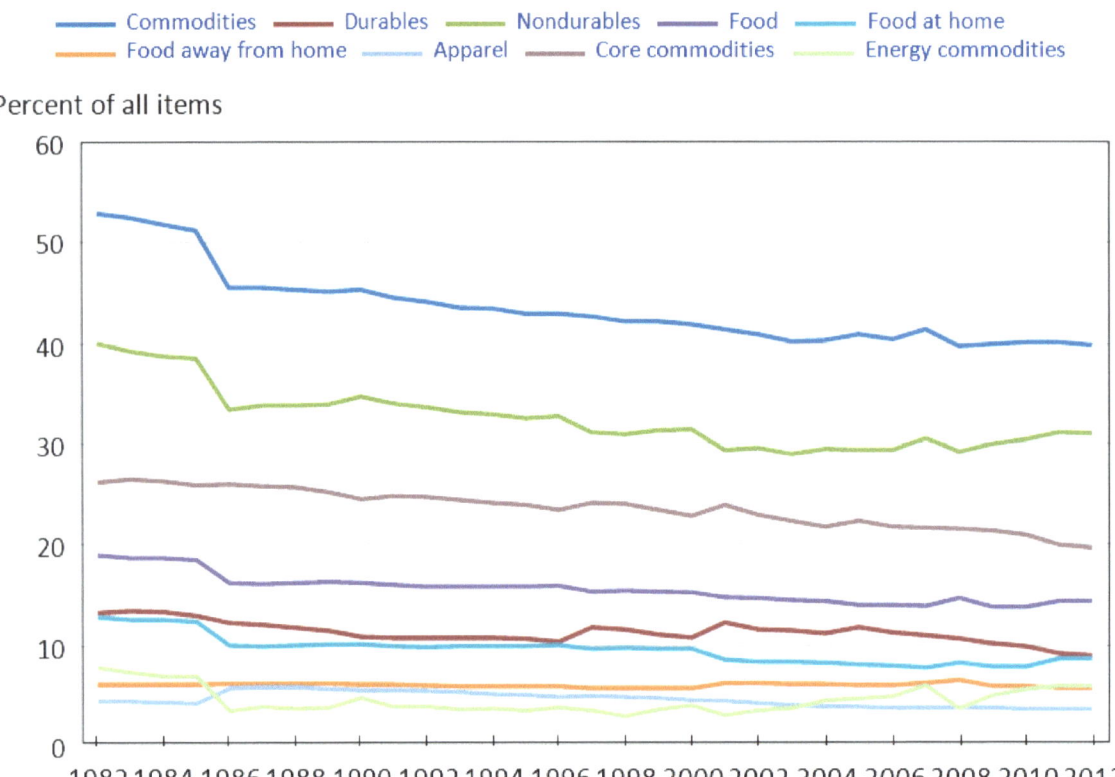

In figure 2, the major standout is shelter, or more specifically, OER. Over the period, the services index and the "core" services index (i.e., "services less energy services") both increase in line with the increase in OER (although there is a downward shift in shelter and OER beginning around 2008), with a larger blip observed from 1985 to 1986. The other larger blips occur in December 1997, when the relative importance of "other services" increased from 7.6 percent to 10.6 percent, while the relative importance of medical care services decreased from 6.1 percent to 4.4 percent. These changes were associated with the introduction in January 1998 of new expenditure weights based on the 1993–1995 CE. Thus, two indexes which appear to drive the increase in the relative importance of the services index are the indexes for OER and "other services."

Figure 2. Relative importance of specific CPI-U service indexes, December 1982–December 2012

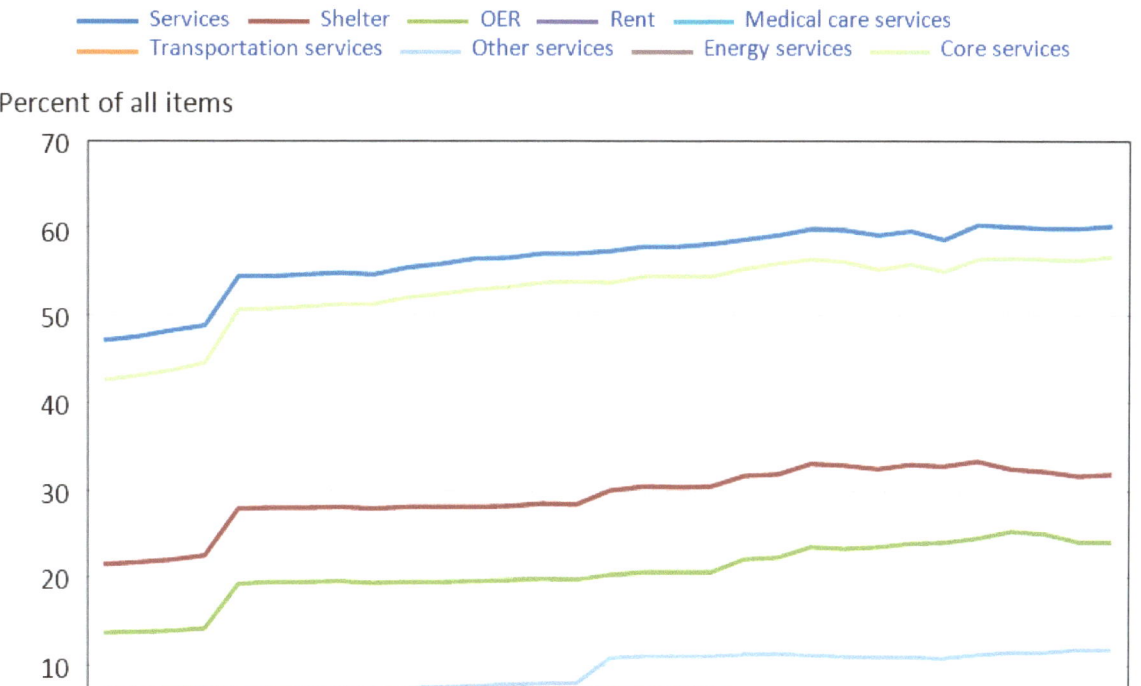

Click legend items to change data display. Hover over chart to view data.
Source: U.S. Bureau of Labor Statistics.

The impact of shelter. The index for shelter, which includes the indexes for "rent of primary residence" and OER, currently represents approximately 32 percent of all expenditures by urban consumers. Figure 2 reveals that, since OER's introduction in the CPI-U, the relative importance of OER has increased from 13.5 percent of total expenditures in December 1982 to 24.0 percent in December 2012; over the same period, the relative importance of rent of primary residence in the CPI-U has increased from 6.0 percent to 6.5 percent (rent of primary residence increased from 5.9 percent to 6.5 percent in the last 2 years of the period, most likely as a result of the recent economic downturn).[31] This shift means that the increase in the relative importance of shelter from 21.3 percent in December 1982 to 31.7 percent in December 2012 has been driven almost entirely by the change in the relative importance of OER. This interpretation is confirmed by figure 3, which shows the relative importances of OER and rent as shares of the overall relative importance of the services index.

Figure 3. Shelter, OER, and rent as shares of the CPI-U services index, December 1982–December 2012

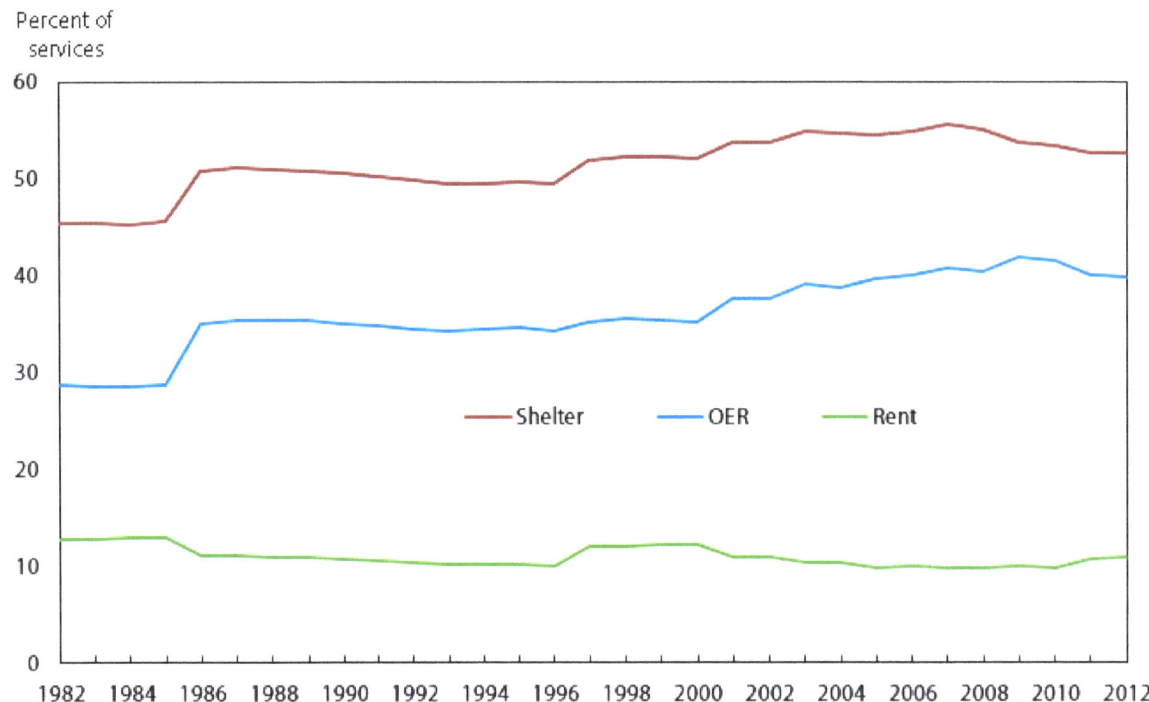

Source: U.S. Bureau of Labor Statistics.

The increase in OER's relative importance from 14.0 percent in December 1985 to 19.1 percent in December 1986 (in figure 3, from 28.7 percent to 35.0 percent of services) deserves an explanation. The OER index was introduced in the CPI-U by BLS in January 1983,[32] and its relative importance set to 13.5 percent. The relative importance was derived from actual CE data collected during the 1972–1973 CE, based on the following question: "If someone were to rent your home today, how much do you think it would rent for monthly, unfurnished and without utilities?"[33] The OER relative importance from 1972–1973 was then updated to December 1982 by relative price change, a procedure not unique to OER (the relative importances of other CPI categories for December 1982 would also have been based on the 1972–1973 survey data and updated by relative price change).[34] As stated by two BLS economists in June 1982, the weight for rental equivalence in December 1982 was "recalculated using the complex statistical estimating procedure used for weights in the official CPI."[35]

However, it must be noted that the relative importance of OER was 15.1 percent based on 1972–1973 CE data and 18.2 percent based on 1982–1984 CE data.[36] Thus, relative expenditures on OER increased, although the relative importance of 13.5 percent, which was obtained when OER was first introduced in December 1982, indicates that relative expenditures on OER declined. This result occurs because the 13.5-percent estimate reflects annual updating of the 1972–1973 relative importances by price indexes during the interval between the 1972–1973 and 1982–1984 updates of expenditure weights. Rents increased at a lower rate than the rate of overall inflation, so the relative weight of OER, as measured by price change, declined, even though the overall quantity of shelter services increased. In other words, the overall jump in the OER weight in December 1986 reflects a considerable increase in the relative quantity of OER, an increase that began in the 1970s. This is an example of how the CPI traditionally picked up major changes in quantity with a lag, namely, as part of major revisions, when new weights were introduced. These lags, and resulting data blips, have been reduced since 2002 with the introduction of new weights every 2 years instead of approximately every 10 years.

While the starting point for this analysis is December 1982, the trends in relative price and quantity should be understood as having been underway as early as the early 1970s. The December 1982 weight update reflects not only the date of OER introduction but also the factors driving the shifts in the 1970s in relative quantity from commodities to services. Indeed, demographic and economic changes in the 1970s help explain the increase in OER quantity and relative importance.[37]

Figure 4. Relative change in price and quantity for "rent of shelter" and "services less rent of shelter," December 1982–December 2012

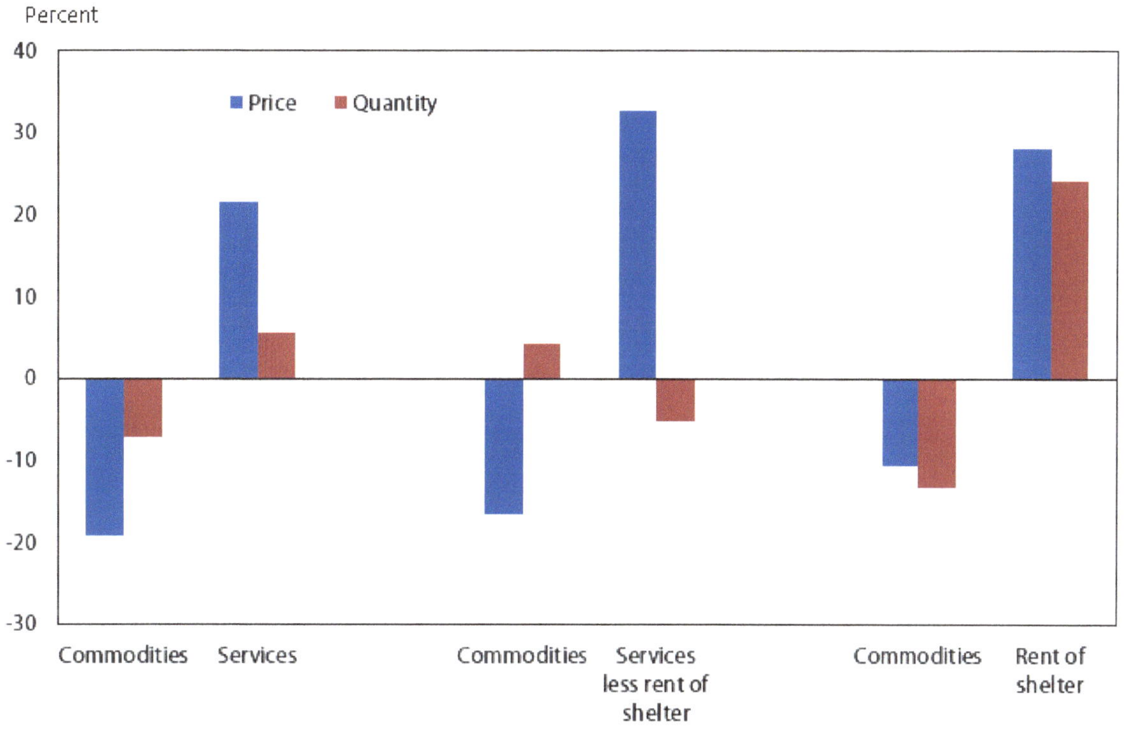

Source: U.S. Bureau of Labor Statistics.

The near doubling in the relative importance of the index for OER, and the accompanying large increase for shelter, warrants an analysis of how the relative shift in expenditures from commodities to services illuminates a relative shift in expenditures from commodities to shelter. Indeed, after accounting for price change, the increase in the quantity of shelter since December 1982 emerges as a major determinant of the shift in quantity from commodities to services. Comparing the indexes for commodities and "services less rent of shelter" reveals that the quantity of commodities increased by 4.2 percent, while the quantity of "services less rent of shelter" decreased by 5.2 percent. Comparing the indexes for commodities and "rent of shelter," however, reverses the results: the quantity of commodities decreased by 13.3 percent, while the quantity of shelter increased by 24.1 percent. These changes are accompanied by a quantity decrease of 7.2 percent for commodities, compared with an increase of 5.4 percent for services. (See figure 4.)[38]

These calculations are straightforward with the use of the officially published index for "rent of shelter." The index is used to calculate the change in expenditure on shelter services that would result exclusively from a change in the price of shelter services. The change in quantity can then be derived from calculations described earlier.[39] Similar calculations comparing commodities with OER show that the quantity of commodities consumed decreased by 15.2 percent, while the quantity of OER consumed increased by 41.8 percent. Meanwhile, the quantity of commodities increased by 4.0 percent from December 1982 to December 2012, while the quantity of "services less OER" (an experimentally constructed index) decreased by 4.0 percent over the same period.[40] (See figure 5.)

Figure 5. Relative change in price and quantity for OER and "services less OER," December 1982–December 2012

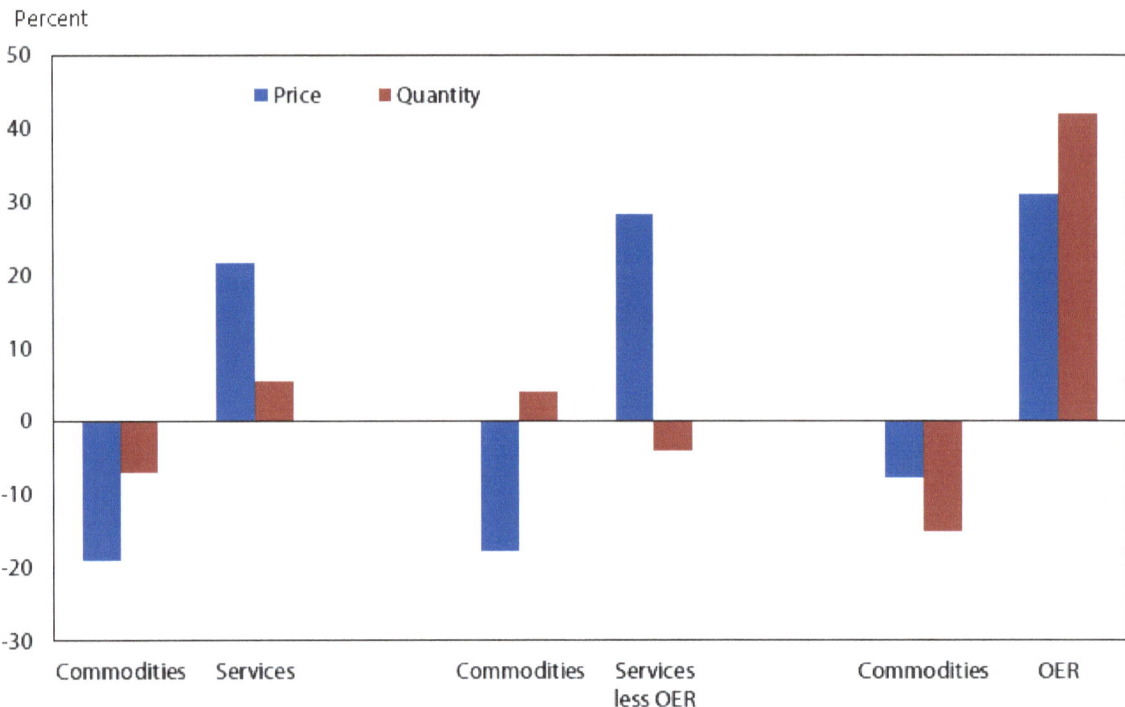

Source: U.S. Bureau of Labor Statistics.

The increase in the quantity of shelter purchased is corroborated by broad trends in the U.S. housing market over the last 30 years; these trends include (1) an increase in the demand for homes, as indicated by a 22-percent increase from 1982 to 2010 (85-percent increase through 2006) in the real home price index compiled by economist Robert Shiller;[41] (2) an increase in the median square footage of floor size of new single-family homes, from 1,520 square feet in 1982 to 2,169 square feet in 2010;[42] and (3) an increase in the homeownership rate, from 65 percent in 1982 to 69 percent in 2005, before a decline to 65 percent in 2012.[43] (These trends are in addition to those noted in endnote 37.)

The impact of nonshelter service categories. Among major service categories other than shelter, medical care services increased in relative importance over the study period, albeit to a lesser degree than shelter, while transportation services and energy services decreased in importance. The share of expenditures that consumers allocated to "other services" (e.g., cable and satellite television and radio service; video cassettes, discs, and other media including rental; and Internet services and electronic information providers) increased from 5.1 percent to 11.6 percent over the period.

As was the case for shelter and OER, the shift in expenditures from commodities to "other services" was not a pure price effect. The quantity of "other services" increased by 56.1 percent over the study period, while the quantity of commodities declined by 9.5 percent; when commodities are compared with "services less other services," the quantity of commodities decreased by only 2.7 percent, while that of "services less other services" increased by 2.3 percent.[44] This shift is not unexpected given the increased availability in the marketplace, over the last quarter century, of such services as cable and satellite television, Internet services, and other digital media capabilities. However, this result contrasts with the finding that the absolute per-household quantity of "other services" declined by 9.1 percent (see table 3), indicating that even as the quantity of "other services" purchased has declined, consumer expenditures on "other services" have come at the expense of commodities, after accounting for relative price change.

Meanwhile, there has been a large relative drop in the quantity of transportation services (an experimental index was created for "services less transportation services") and medical care services, and a slight increase in the quantity of energy services. In short, the composition of consumption has entailed an increase in the quantity of a more diverse set of marketplace offerings and a decrease in the quantity of traditional categories like transportation and medical care, and slightly more of energy services. (Table 5 summarizes these results.)

Table 5. Summary of relative changes in price and quantity, commodities vs. services, December 1982–December 2012 (in percent)

Category	Change in relative expenditure	Change in relative price	Change in relative quantity
Commodities	-25.00	-19.17	-7.21
Services	28.09	21.54	5.39
Commodities	-13.00	-16.52	4.21
Services less rent of shelter	25.72	32.67	-5.24
Commodities	-22.63	-10.78	-13.29
Rent of shelter	58.88	28.04	24.08
Commodities	-14.58	-17.86	3.99
Services less OER	22.96	28.13	-4.03
Commodities	-21.85	-7.89	-15.16
OER	85.70	30.93	41.83
Commodities	-19.41	-17.16	-2.72
Services less other services	24.44	21.60	2.33
Commodities	-15.29	-6.36	-9.54
Other services	159.91	66.48	56.12
Commodities	-25.81	-17.88	-9.66
Services less transportation services	33.95	23.51	8.45
Commodities	-1.54	-5.49	4.19
Transportation services	11.87	42.36	-21.42
Commodities	-24.66	-16.11	-10.19

Category	Change in relative expenditure	Change in relative price	Change in relative quantity
Services less medical care services	31.01	20.26	8.94
Commodities	-3.73	-11.10	8.28
Medical care services	39.33	116.97	-35.78
Commodities	-25.70	-19.71	-7.46
Services less energy services	32.04	24.58	6.00
Commodities	-0.62	-0.22	-0.41
Energy services	7.09	2.49	4.49

Source: U.S. Bureau of Labor Statistics and author's calculations.

The large relative drop in medical care services comes as a surprise, but it is important to recall the distinction between total consumption expenditures and consumption attributed to out-of-pocket expenditures on medical care services. The CPI is a measure of the average change over time in the prices paid for a constant-quality market basket of goods and services. The CPI, then, is a measure of consumption derived from out-of-pocket expenditures and not necessarily a measure of total consumption. As explained earlier, it is indeed the case that total expenditures on medical care services for the benefit of consumers have increased, while consumer out-of-pocket expenditures on medical care services have decreased; as a result, the quantity of medical care services paid for out of pocket has decreased relative to that of commodities.

Figure 6. Durables and nondurables as shares of the CPI-U for commodities, December 1982–December 2012

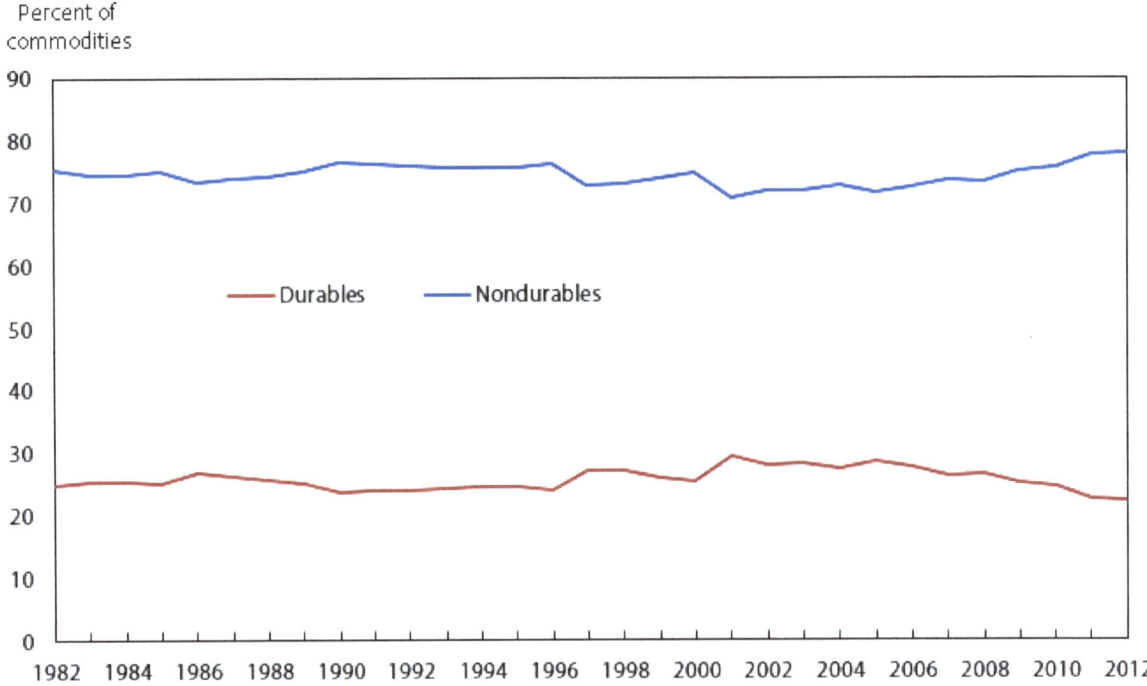

Source: U.S. Bureau of Labor Statistics.

Durables versus nondurables. Additional insight into long-term changes in the composition of expenditures can be obtained by disaggregating commodities into durables and nondurables. Figure 6 shows that the relative importances of durables (e.g., appliances, new vehicles, televisions, and sporting goods) and nondurables (e.g., food, apparel, medical care commodities, and motor fuel), calculated as shares of the relative importance for the CPI-U index for commodities, have remained relatively stable over the period. But a closer look at the price and quantity effects of these changes in expenditures reveals that consumers have purchased relatively more durables than nondurables, as they have shifted to more services. Thus, the general result of a shift from commodities to shelter remains unchanged. Further, regardless of whether durables and nondurables are compared with services or with "services less rent of shelter" and "rent of shelter," consumers have increased their purchases of durable goods while reducing their purchases of nondurables.

Figure 7. Relative change in price and quantity for durables, nondurables, and "rent of shelter," December 1982–December 2012

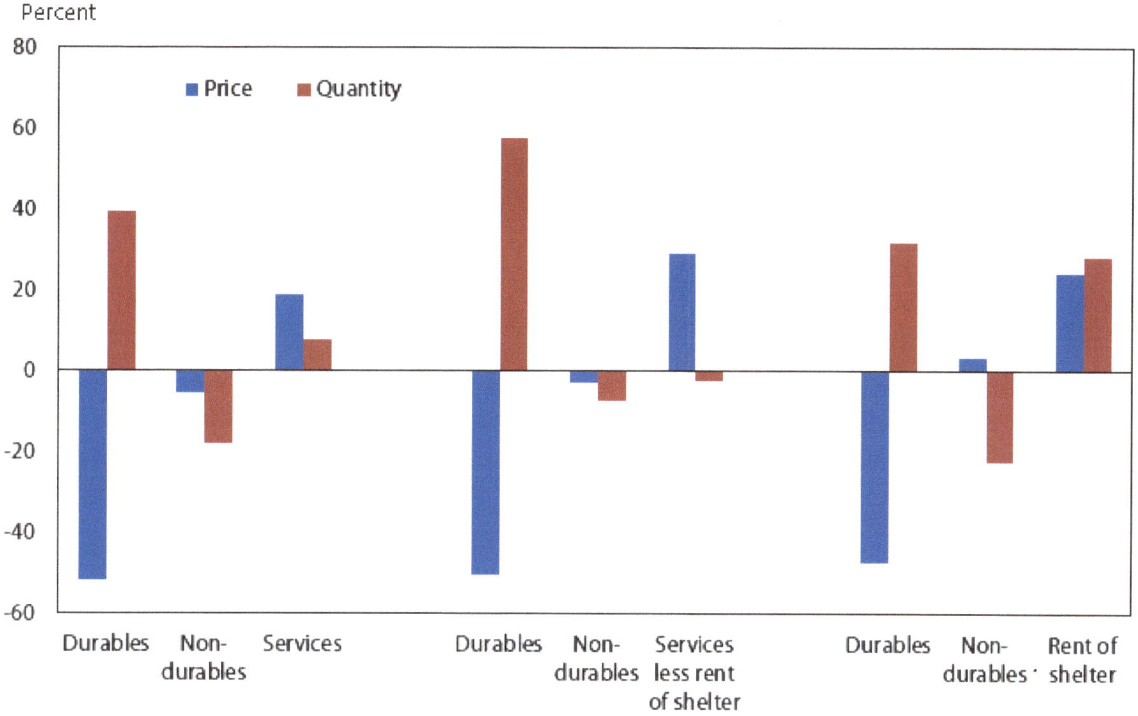

Source: U.S. Bureau of Labor Statistics.

Comparing commodities with "services less rent of shelter" reveals that, from December 1982 to December 2012, the quantity of items purchased increased by 57.6 percent for commodities, decreased by 7.2 percent for nondurables, and decreased by 2.6 percent for "services less rent of shelter." A similar comparison of commodities with "rent of shelter" shows that, over the same period, the quantity of durables increased by 31.7 percent, that of nondurables decreased by 22.5 percent, and that of "rent of shelter" increased by 28.0 percent. (See figure 7.) Similar results can be obtained when comparing durables and nondurables against OER. (See figure 8.) This finding may reflect increased purchases of durable goods, as well as shelter, after traditional necessities like food and clothing have been covered.

Figure 8. Relative change in price and quantity for durables, nondurables, and OER, December 1982–December 2012

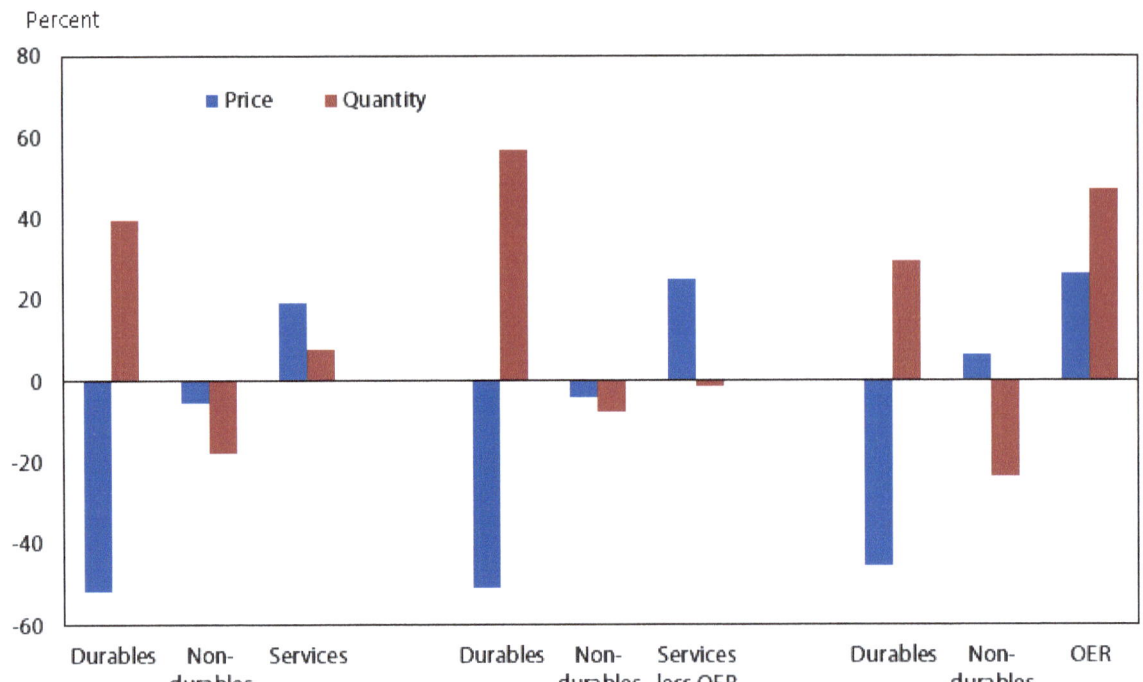

Source: U.S. Bureau of Labor Statistics.

None of these findings indicates that the absolute consumption of any particular category of goods and services has decreased. The analysis pertains to *relative* changes in quantity. The increase in the quantity of durables relative to nondurables does not mean that consumers buy less food and clothing. Durable commodities comprised only 8.8 percent of total consumer expenditures in 2012, compared with 13.1 percent in 1982; nondurable commodities comprised 31.0 percent of expenditures in 2012, compared with 39.9 percent in 1982. Consumers still spend more on nondurable items such as food and clothing than on durable items like televisions and cars, but nondurables have become relatively less important in the overall market basket of goods and services.

Clearly, then, not only has a shift in consumption occurred between commodities and shelter, but the quantity of durables has increased while the quantity of nondurables has decreased—a result that holds regardless of the overall increase in the consumption of shelter. To the extent that the decline in the relative quantity of nondurables might reflect a decline in the quantity of medical care commodities, it should be recalled that CPI expenditure data reflect out-of-pocket expenditures. A decline in the quantity of medical care commodities does not necessarily imply less consumption of medical care commodities; it implies only that an increase in consumption (as might be reflected in PCE data) is covered by employer-provided and other third-party health care insurance premium support.

A similar outcome occurs when comparing durables and nondurables with major categories of services. As shown above, from December 1982 to December 2012, the quantity of shelter, "other services," and energy services increased relative to commodities, while consumption of transportation services and medical care services decreased. Further, it is observed that consumption increased for durable goods, decreased for nondurable goods, increased significantly for shelter and "other services," increased less significantly for energy services, and decreased for transportation services and medical care services. (Table 6 summarizes the results.)

Table 6. Summary of relative changes in price and quantity, durables and nondurables vs. services, December 1982–December 2012 (in percent)

Category	Change in relative expenditure	Change in relative price	Change in relative quantity
Durables	-32.92	-51.89	39.43
Nondurables	-22.41	-5.46	-17.92
Services	28.09	19.01	7.63
Durables	-22.19	-50.62	57.56
Nondurables	-9.99	-2.96	-7.25
Services less rent of shelter	25.72	29.11	-2.63
Durables	-30.81	-47.45	31.67
Nondurables	-19.96	3.26	-22.49
Rent of shelter	58.88	24.07	28.05
Durables	-23.60	-51.29	56.83
Nondurables	-11.63	-4.28	-7.68
Services less OER	22.96	25.01	-1.64
Durables	-30.10	-45.98	29.38
Nondurables	-19.15	6.16	-23.84
OER	85.70	26.32	47.01
Durables	-27.92	-50.77	46.42
Nondurables	-16.62	-3.27	-13.81
Services less other services	24.44	18.87	4.68
Durables	-24.24	-45.40	38.75
Nondurables	-12.36	7.30	-18.32
Other services	159.91	59.70	62.75
Durables	-33.65	-51.21	36.00
Nondurables	-23.24	-4.13	-19.94
Services less transportation services	33.95	20.71	10.96

Category	Change in relative expenditure	Change in relative price	Change in relative quantity
Durables	-11.94	-44.85	59.67
Nondurables	1.87	8.38	-6.01
Transportation services	11.87	36.68	-18.15
Durables	-32.62	-50.16	35.21
Nondurables	-22.05	-2.07	-20.41
Services less medical care services	31.01	17.53	11.47
Durables	-13.90	-48.05	65.75
Nondurables	-0.40	2.07	-2.42
Medical care services	39.33	108.55	-33.19
Durables	-33.55	-52.25	39.18
Nondurables	-23.13	-6.17	-18.07
Services less energy services	32.04	21.88	8.34
Durables	-11.12	-41.99	53.22
Nondurables	2.81	13.99	-9.80
Energy Services	7.09	-1.98	9.25

Source: U.S. Bureau of Labor Statistics and author's calculations.

THE U.S. ECONOMY HAS CHANGED from being a manufacturing-based economy to being one based largely on services production. This change has been accompanied by a shift in the allocation of consumer expenditures from commodities to services, despite a relative decrease in the prices of commodities. This article has examined the price and quantity components of changes in expenditures to identify the particular categories of services driving the overall shift to services consumption. Focusing on absolute changes in per-household expenditures during the 1984–2011 period, the article found a 9.1-percent increase in the quantity of services and no change in the quantity of commodities. This trend has been driven by an 18.5-percent increase in the quantity of shelter and a 20.2-percent increase in the quantity of OER. Meanwhile, the absolute quantity of durable goods has increased, while the absolute quantity of nondurable goods has decreased. The quantity of health care services decreased by 17.8 percent, although the share of PCE accounted for by health care services increased from 4.7 percent in 1959 to 16.2 percent in 2009. This difference occurs because PCE data account for third-party expenditures, while CE and CPI data account only for out-of-pocket expenditures.

Focusing on relative expenditures for the 30-year period from December 1982 to December 2012, the analysis found an increase in the total quantity of services at the expense of commodities—a shift primarily driven by an increase in the quantity of shelter, in particular owner-occupied shelter. This shift has paralleled an increase in housing demand and homeownership rates over most of the last three decades, as well as an increase in the size of new single-family homes. The analysis also found that the quantity of energy services and "other services" has increased relative to commodities, while the quantity of transportation services and medical care services has decreased. The decrease in quantity of medical care services does not mean that consumers have consumed less medical care services; rather, it means that third-party premium support has picked up the tab.

In addition, the quantity of durable goods has increased relative to nondurable goods. This shift from nondurable to durable commodities is observed regardless of whether durables and nondurables are compared with "rent of shelter" or "services less rent of shelter." This result also holds when comparing durables and nondurables with OER, "other services," transportation services, medical care services, and energy services. In short, CPI and CE data show that the shift to a services-based economy entails more and bigger homes, more of "other services" (such as Internet services and cable television) relative to commodities, more durable items, and more energy services in 2012 than in 1982, while PCE data indicate that total consumption expenditures on health care and financial services have increased.

Appendix

Table A–1. Mapping of CE items to CPI special aggregate categories, 1984 and 2011

Special aggregate	1984	2011
Commodities	Durables and nondurables	Durables and nondurables
Services	Shelter, transportation services, medical care services, energy services, other services, water and sewerage maintenance, trash and garbage collection, household operations, miscellaneous	Shelter, transportation services, medical care services, energy services, other services, water and sewerage maintenance, trash and garbage collection, household operations, miscellaneous
Shelter	Rent and "Estimated monthly rental value of owned home" (excludes other lodging)	Rent and "Estimated monthly rental value of owned home" (excludes other lodging)
Transportation services	Maintenance and repairs,[1] vehicle insurance, vehicle rental licenses and other charges, public transportation	Maintenance and repairs;[2] vehicle insurance; vehicle rental, leases, licenses, and other charges; public and other transportation
Health care services	Health insurance and medical services[3]	Health insurance and medical services[4]
Energy services	Natural gas and electricity	Natural gas and electricity
Other services	Telephone; apparel services;[5] postage; fees and admissions; video cassettes, tapes, and discs; rental of televisions; rental of VCR, radio, and sound equipment; rental of video cassettes, tapes, discs, and films; pet services; veterinary services; film processing; repair and rental of photographic equipment; photographer fees; personal care services; education services,[6] miscellaneous[7]	Telephone services; apparel service;[8] postage and delivery services; fees and admissions; cable and satellite television; satellite radio service; online gaming services; video cassettes, tapes, and discs; streaming, downloading video; applications, games, ringtones for handheld devices; rental of televisions; streaming, downloading audio; rental of VCR, radio, and sound equipment; rental and repair of musical instruments; rental of video cassettes, tapes, films, and discs; rental of computer and video game hardware and software; rental of video hardware and accessories; rental of video software; pet services; veterinary services; photo processing; repair and rental of photographic equipment; photographer fees; personal care services; education services;[9] miscellaneous[10]
Durables	Household furnishings and equipment;[11] vehicle purchases;[12] transportation maintenance and repair supplies;[13] televisions; VCRs, video disc players; video games hardware and software; radios; phonographs; tape recorders and players; sound components and component systems; miscellaneous sound equipment; sound equipment accessories; un-motored boats and trailers; powered sports vehicles; outboard motors; sports equipment[14]	Household furnishings and equipment;[15] vehicle purchases;[16] transportation maintenance and repair supplies;[17] radios; phonographs; televisions; tape recorders and players; miscellaneous sound equipment; miscellaneous video equipment; sound equipment accessories; VCRs and video disc players; digital media players and recorders; video game hardware and software; video game software; video game hardware and accessories; personal digital audio players; sound components and component systems; satellite dishes; motored and un-motored recreational vehicles; outboard motors; sports, recreation, and exercise equipment[18]

Special aggregate	1984	2011
Nondurables	Food at home; food away from home; fuel oil and other fuels; termite and pest control products; housekeeping supplies; stationery, stationery supplies, gift wrap; floor covering; window covering; apparel; gasoline and motor oil; prescription and nonprescription drugs; medical supplies;[19] records, tapes, needles, styli; musical instruments and accessories; pet food; pet purchases, supplies, medicine; toys, games, hobbies, and tricycles; playground equipment; film; other photographic supplies; photographic equipment; fireworks, souvenirs, visual goods, pinball, electronic video games; personal care products; reading materials; school books, supplies for day care, nursery, other; school books, supplies for college and for elementary and high school; tobacco products and smoking supplies	Food at home; food away from home; fuel oil and other fuels; termite and pest control products; housekeeping supplies; stationery, stationery supplies, gift wrap; floor covering; window covering; apparel; gasoline and motor oil; prescription and nonprescription drugs; medical supplies;[20] CDs, records, audio tapes; musical instruments and accessories; pet food; pet purchase, supplies, medicine; toys, games, arts and crafts, and tricycles; stamp and coin collecting; playground equipment; film; other photographic supplies; photographic equipment; fireworks; souvenirs; visual goods; pinball, electronic video games; personal care products; reading materials; school books, supplies, equipment; tobacco products and smoking supplies

Notes:

[1] Not including coolant, brake fluid, transmission fluid, additives, tires, parts, equipment and accessories, and vehicle products.

[2] Not including coolant, brake fluid, transmission fluid, other additives, tires, parts, equipment and accessories, vehicle audio equipment, and vehicle video equipment.

[3] Physician's services, dental services, eye care services, service by professionals other than physicians, lab tests, x-rays, nurse services, hospital services, etc.

[4] Physician's services, dental services, eye care services, service by professionals other than physicians, lab tests, x-rays, hospital services, etc.

[5] Shoe repair, other shoe service; coin-operated apparel laundry and dry cleaning; apparel alteration and repair; clothing rental; watch and jewelry repair; apparel laundry and dry cleaning not coin operated; and clothing storage.

[6] College tuition, elementary and high school tuition, other school tuition, and other school expenses including rentals.

[7] Miscellaneous fees, pari-mutuel losses, legal fees, funeral expenses, safety deposit box rental, checking accounts, other bank services, cemetery lots or vaults, accounting fees, miscellaneous personal services, finance charges excluding mortgage vehicle, and occupational expenses.

[8] Shoe repair and other shoe service; coin-operated apparel laundry and dry cleaning; alteration, repair, and tailoring of apparel and accessories; clothing rental; watch and jewelry repair; apparel laundry and dry cleaning not coin-operated; and clothing storage.

[9] College tuition, elementary and high school tuition, vocational and technical school tuition, test preparation, tutoring services, other schools tuition, and other school expenses including rentals.

[10] Lotteries and pari-mutuel losses, legal fees, funeral expenses, safe deposit box rental, checking accounts, other bank service charges, cemetery lots, vaults, maintenance fees, accounting fees, miscellaneous personal services, dating services, finance charges excluding mortgage and vehicle, occupational expenses, expenses for other properties, interest paid on home equity line of credit, credit card memberships, shopping club membership fees, and vacation clubs.

[11] Not including floor coverings and window coverings.

[12] New cars and trucks, used cars and trucks, and other vehicles.

[13] Coolant, brakes, transmission fluid, additives, tires, parts, equipment and accessories, and vehicle products.

[14] Not including rental and repair of miscellaneous sports equipment.

[15] Not including floor coverings and window coverings.

[16] New cars and trucks, used cars and trucks, and other vehicles.

[17] Coolant, brake fluid, transmission fluid, other additives, tires, parts, equipment and accessories, vehicle audio equipment, and vehicle video equipment.

Not including rental and repair of miscellaneous sports equipment.

(19) Not including rental of medical equipment.

(20) Not including rental of medical equipment and rental of supportive, convalescent medical equipment.

Source: U.S. Bureau of Labor Statistics.

Notes

1 When discussing changes in quantity, this article refers to a residual between changes in expenditures and changes in price. In this interpretation, consumers buy "more" or "less" of a category of commodity or service, depending on whether the change in quantity is positive or negative.

2 The CPI program defines an index and expenditure category for "medical care services." The CE program defines an expenditure category for "health care services." The PCE program defines an index and expenditure category for "health care services." The CE expenditure category and the CPI index and expenditure category "consist only of those services directly purchased by consumers." The PCE index and expenditure category "include those services directly purchased by consumers and those services paid for on behalf of consumers." See Clinton P. McCully, Brian C. Moyer, and Kenneth J. Stewart, "A reconciliation between the Consumer Price Index and the Personal Consumption Expenditures price index" (U.S. Bureau of Economic Analysis and U.S. Bureau of Labor Statistics, September 2007), p. 12, http://www.bea.gov/papers/pdf/cpi_pce.pdf. This article treats "medical care services" and "health care services" as conceptually the same thing.

3 Victor R. Fuchs, assisted by Irving F. Leveson, "The service economy" (UMI, 1968), p. 1, http://www.nber.org/chapters/c1155.pdf.

4 The shift from goods to services has probably been greater and swifter on the production side because of the tremendous growth in imported goods.

5 The CE estimates amount to a 40-percent share for commodities and 60-percent share for services in 2011, compared with a 60–40 split in 2012 based on CPI relative importance data. Thus, no discrepancy results from how this article classifies all CE expenditures relative to how the cost weight section of the CPI classifies CE expenditures for purposes of the CPI. For historical BLS relative importance tables, which can be obtained online back to 1986, see http://www.bls.gov/cpi.

6 Clinton P. McCully, "Trends in consumer spending and personal saving, 1959–2009," *Survey of Current Business* (U.S. Bureau of Economic Analysis, June 2011), p. 15, http://www.bea.gov/scb/pdf/2011/06%20June/0611_pce.pdf.

7 Ibid., p. 15.

8 The index for shelter is comprised primarily of the indexes for "rent of primary residence" and "owners' equivalent rent." The index for "owners' equivalent rent" was introduced in the CPI-U in January 1983 (with base period December 1982 = 100) and in the CPI-W in January 1985 (with base period December 1984 = 100).

9 The CPI measures price change for 211 item categories (e.g., cereals and bakery products) in 38 geographic areas (e.g., Boston–Brockton–Nashua), forming 8,018 basic item-area index cells (211x38) that serve as the building blocks from which aggregate indexes are constructed. For example, six item categories (cereals and bakery products; meats, poultry, fish, and eggs; dairy and related products; fruits and vegetables; nonalcoholic beverages and beverage materials; and other food at home) make up the index for food at home. As one illustration, the food-at-home index can be computed for the Boston–Brockton–Nashua metropolitan area, for a set of cities that make up the Northeast urban geographic area, and for all cities in which prices are collected to form an index at the level of the U.S. City Average. In

total, the CPI consists of thousands of indexes that measure price change for narrow and broad categories of goods and services across multiple geographic areas.

[10] Each month, BLS sends approximately 400 economic assistants (EAs) to 87 urban areas in the United States to collect prices on approximately 80,000 goods and services. EAs collect information on rents from approximately 7,000 housing units (through the Housing Survey) and prices from approximately 26,000 outlets (through the C&S Survey), including supermarkets, department stores, car dealerships, and other retail establishments. The Telephone Point of Purchase Survey (TPOPS) provides a mechanism to ensure that the market basket of approximately 80,000 goods and services is regularly updated to capture changes over time in the specific places consumers shop and the specific goods and services they purchase. Conducted quarterly, TPOPS "furnishes data on retail outlets from which metropolitan and urban nonmetropolitan households purchased defined groups of commodities and services to be priced in the CPI" (*BLS handbook of methods*, chapter 17 (U.S. Bureau of Labor Statistics, last updated July 2013), p. 13, http://www.bls.gov/opub/hom/pdf/homch17.pdf). Over the course of 4 years, TPOPS identifies a completely new set of retail establishments in which consumers currently buy goods and services in the marketplace (although the new set may contain many of the same establishments from a previous sample). Once outlets are selected, EAs visit the outlets and conduct price initiation, followed by monthly (or bimonthly) price collection. If items are no longer sold in the outlets, EAs employ a set of rules to select the most equivalent item as a replacement for the discontinued item, in order to continue pricing. If deemed more efficient, some prices are collected from sources other than the C&S Survey. The Housing Survey is also designed to update the set of housing units from which rent prices are collected.

11 *BLS handbook of methods*, chapter 17 (U.S. Bureau of Labor Statistics, last updated July 2013), p. 13.

12 Between weight updates based on new CE data, expenditure allocations are updated on the basis of the relative change in the price indexes for each category of expenditure. Beginning in April 2012, BLS publishes monthly updates of the relative importance of items in the CPI.

13 CE data used in this article reflect expenditures by all consumers, urban and rural. CPI indexes used to deflate expenditures reflect only expenditures by urban consumers. Line-by-line comparisons of the percent differences in 1988 expenditures for all and for urban-only consumers show differences of less than 10 percent, although for some items, such as coal or propane gas, the differences are larger. The CE data for line-by-line comparisons are for 1988 because the CE for 1984 did not collect data from rural consumers.

14 The two major categories of commodities, durables and nondurables, show respective expenditures of $3,338 and $7,053 in 1984, and $4,819 and $13,588 in 2011. In both years, the sum of expenditures on durables and nondurables is equal to total expenditures on commodities ($10,292 in 1984 and $18,408 in 2011), except for rounding. However, the major categories of services (rent of shelter, other services, transportation services, medical care services, and energy services) make up approximately 95 percent of total expenditures on services in 1984 and 94 percent in 2011. The remaining expenditures on services consist of expenditures on water and sewerage maintenance, trash and garbage collection, household operations, and other miscellaneous items.

15 The CE data on shelter contain data on "owned dwellings," that is, data on mortgage interest, insurance, repairs, and many other items that conflate consumption and investment. However, the CE also collects data on the estimated monthly rental value of an owned home, as well as residential rent. This article excludes all data under shelter, except residential rent and the estimated monthly rental value of an owned home, thus aligning the CE data with CPI relative importance tables; it excludes expenditures on "other lodging" because such expenditures also conflate consumption and investment.

16 See U.S. Census Bureau data at http://www.census.gov/const/C25Ann/sftotalmedavgsqft.pdf.

17 The category "other services" includes cable and satellite television and radio service, rental of video or audio discs and other media, pet services, veterinary services, photographers and film processing, other recreation services (club membership dues, fees for participant sports and group exercises, admissions (movies, concerts, sporting events, etc.), and fees for lessons or instructions), tuition, postage and delivery services, telephone services (wireless telephone services and land-line telephone services), Internet services and electronic information providers, personal care services (haircuts and other personal care services), miscellaneous personal services (legal fees, funeral expenses, laundry and dry cleaning services, other apparel services (shoe repair, alterations, and watch and jewelry repair), financial services (checking accounts and other bank services, and tax return preparation)), and unsampled photography.

18 McCully, "Trends in consumer spending and personal saving," p. 15.

19 Ibid., pp. 15–16.

20 Ibid., p. 16.

21 Major advances in medical care technology, such as surgical procedures, new prescription drugs, and medical devices such as CT scanners "have in general been quite expensive and have contributed significantly to the growth in health costs. Research on this issue has generally concluded that around half of the growth in per household inflation-adjusted health expenditures is attributable to advances in medical technology" (McCully, "Trends in consumer spending and personal saving," p. 17).

22 From 1959 to 2009, there has been a "large increase in the share of PCE accounted for by services, particularly by health care and by financial services and insurance" (McCully, "Trends in consumer spending and personal saving," p. 14). Thus, while total consumption expenditures on health care services increased as a share of total consumption expenditures on all services, a decreasing share of these expenditures was covered out of pocket by consumers.

[23] According to its entry level item (ELI) definition, the checking accounts and other bank services category includes fees related to checking accounts and checking-type accounts, fees for safe deposit boxes, and annual fees for credit cards. Fees related to checking-type accounts include monthly (or other periodic) charges for the maintenance of an account; transaction charges; the cost of personalized checks; charges for cashier's, certified, or traveler's checks; charges for money orders; charges for notaries public; and other charges (such as ATM fees) related to checking account type services. The category of tax return preparation and other accounting fees includes all charges for the time and expertise taken to prepare the required tax forms necessary for filing an individual's personal income tax return. Other accounting fees have been truncated from pricing for this ELI.

[24] McCully, "Trends in consumer spending and personal saving," p. 17.

[25] The full set of durable goods includes furniture and bedding; appliances; other household equipment and furnishings; tools, hardware, outdoor equipment and supplies; new vehicles; used cars and trucks; un-sampled new and used motor vehicles; motor vehicle parts and equipment; televisions; other video equipment; audio equipment; sporting goods; personal computers and peripheral equipment; computer software and accessories; and telephone hardware, calculators, and other consumer information items.

[26] The full set of nondurables includes food; alcoholic beverages; apparel; fuel oil and other fuels; window and floor coverings; housekeeping supplies; motor fuel; medical care commodities; audio discs, tapes, and other media; un-sampled video and audio; pets and pet products; photographic equipment and supplies; recreational reading materials; other recreational goods; educational books and supplies; tobacco and smoking products; personal care products; and miscellaneous personal goods.

[27] McCully, "Trends in consumer spending and personal saving," p. 15.

[28] The CPI medical care index does include expenditures by the government as part of the Medicare Part B, C, and D programs.

[29] For a review of the differences between CPI and PCE, see McCully et al., "A reconciliation between the Consumer Price Index and the Personal Consumption Expenditures price index."

[30] Before the introduction of new expenditure weights in December 1997, the apparel index was known as the "apparel and upkeep" index and consisted of apparel commodities and apparel services (laundry, dry cleaning, and other apparel services). Relative importance for apparel commodities is used in the years before 1997.

[31] See CPI relative importance table for December 2012 at www.bls.gov/cpi. See also *CPI detailed report*, table 1, December 1982.

[32] See "Changing the homeownership component of the Consumer Price Index to rental equivalence," in *CPI detailed report*, January 1983; and Robert Gillingham and Walter Lane, "Changing the treatment of shelter costs for homeowners in the CPI," *Monthly Labor Review*, June 1982, p. 9, http://www.bls.gov/opub/mlr/1982/06/art2full.pdf. See also "Treatment of homeownership in the CPI," PowerPoint presentation prepared by Frank Ptacek. Before December 1982, the homeownership component of the CPI tracked changes in house prices, mortgage interest rates, property taxes, insurance, and maintenance costs. This treatment failed to distinguish between investment in the stock of housing and consumption of the flow of shelter services associated with housing. A 1961 report by George Stigler titled "The price statistics of the federal government" (National Bureau of Economic Research, 1961), also known as the Stigler report, criticized this treatment and advocated a flow-of-services approach to measuring the value of housing. The report, available at http://www.nber.org/chapters/c6484.pdf, stated that "the welfare of consumers depends on the flow of services from durable goods, not upon the stocks acquired in a given period" (p. 53). Just as the CPI excluded changes in the value of stocks and bonds, the Stigler report argued that the change in the asset value of the house, and the cost of equity in holding that asset, should be excluded from the CPI; the CPI should only measure the change

in the cost of shelter provided by the house. Motivated by the report, BLS research and analysis on the use of a flow-of-services concept for measuring price change in owner-occupied housing began in 1970 and continued throughout the decade.

33 See "Treatment of homeownership in the CPI," PowerPoint presentation prepared by Frank Ptacek; and "Treatment of homeownership in the CPI: a historical perspective with a view to the future," PowerPoint presentation prepared by Frank Ptacek, February 27, 2004. See also *CPI detailed report*, January 1983, p. 9: "In the 1972–73 CE survey, each homeowner was asked: 'If you were to rent out your home today, how much do you think it would rent for monthly, unfurnished and without utilities?' Studies of the responses to this question showed estimates to be reasonable. The responses, tabulated by geographic area, structure type, age, and other variables, were compared, cell by cell, with the rents on similarly classified renter-occupied residences. The estimated rents for owner units were, consistently, slightly higher than the actual rents for the renter units. This indicates that it is likely that owner-occupied homes are, as is generally thought, somewhat better than those occupied by renters even in the same geographic areas and the same age and structure type categories. Therefore, they command a higher rent."

34 Charles Mason and Clifford Butler, "New basket of goods and services being priced in revised CPI," *Monthly Labor Review*, January 1987, pp. 3–22, especially footnote 11 and discussion on p. 5, http://www.bls.gov/opub/mlr/1987/01/art1full.pdf. The general methodology for updating the OER weight by price change from the 1972–1973 CE to December 1982 was essentially the same as the methodology used for updating the OER weight from the 1982–1984 CE to December 1986. However, "when initially introduced, the 'rental equivalence' index was moved (that is, changes were applied) by reweighting the rent sample to represent owner-occupied units. The preferred methodology would have been to match owner units to renter units and use those more specific rent changes to calculate changes in the rental value of owner units. The reweighting approach was taken because an owner sample could not be selected and available for use before the CPI was last revised in 1987" (Frank Ptacek and Robert M. Baskin, "Revision of the CPI housing sample and estimators," *Monthly Labor Review*, December 1996, pp. 31–32, http://www.bls.gov/opub/mlr/1996/12/art5full.pdf). In sum, the derivation of the December 1982 relative importance for OER was based on methodological procedures employed in the official CPI.

35 Gillingham and Lane, "Changing the treatment of shelter costs for homeowners in the CPI," p. 14.

36 Mason and Butler, "New basket of goods and services," table 3.

37 Demographic characteristics of the urban populations surveyed in the 1972–1973 CE and the 1982–1984 CE indicate that income before taxes increased from $12,332 to $23,183, an increase of 88 percent, while per-household income before taxes increased from $4,404 to $8,917, an increase of 102 percent (inflation measured by the CPI-U, however, increased by 114 percent). Moreover, the percent of the surveyed urban population reporting homeownership increased from 55.8 percent to 59.5 percent (the overall homeownership rate in the United States increased only slightly, from 64.5 percent in 1972–1973 to 64.6 percent in 1982–1984). See Mason and Butler, "New basket of goods and services," table 1. See also http://www.census.gov/housing/hvs/data/histtabs.html.

The increase in the homeownership rate was accompanied by a 26-percent increase in housing inventory from 1972–1973 to 1982–1984, a 43-percent increase in inflation-adjusted median home values in the 1970s, and an increase in real home prices during the 1970s. See http://www.census.gov/hhes/www/housing/census/historic/values.html and http://www.census.gov/housing/hvs/data/histtabs.html. See also Morris A. Davis, Francois Ortalo-Magne, and Peter Rupert, "What's really happening in housing markets?" table 1 (Federal Reserve Bank of Cleveland, July 2007), http://www.clevelandfed.org/research/commentary/2007/07.pdf; and Karl E. Case, "Land prices and house prices in the United States," table 2.1, in Yukio Noguchi and James Poterba, eds., *Housing Markets in the U.S. and Japan* (University of Chicago Press, January 1994), http://www.nber.org/chapters/c8820.pdf.

Added pressure on rental value might have come from a decline in residential vacancy rates. Between 1972–1973 and 1982–1984, residential vacancy rates declined from 4.2 percent to 3.7 percent for one-unit rentals, from 7.0 percent to 6.6 percent for rentals of two or more units, and from 8.2 percent to 7.0 percent for rentals of five or more units. See U.S. Census Bureau data at http://www.census.gov/housing/hvs/data/histtabs.html.

It is worth noting that the 1970s would be the first decade to see a major influx of demand in the housing market from the baby-boom generation.

[38] Note that the price of commodities is observed to decrease in figure 4. It is important to recall that these figures illustrate changes in *relative* price and quantity. Although the absolute prices of commodities and services have increased over time, the prices of commodities have increased at a lower rate than the prices of services, indicating that commodities have become cheaper in comparison with services. The amount of the change in relative price is indicated in the figure.

39 These calculations involve updating the expenditure weight for "rent of shelter," rather than "shelter," because the indexes for "rent of shelter" and "services less rent of shelter" are used to update the weights before normalization and then deflate normalized expenditures to obtain the change in quantity. In the previous section, absolute expenditures on "shelter" and "services less shelter" are used because CE data do not have comparable categories called "rent of shelter" and "services less rent of shelter;" however, these expenditures are then deflated with the use of the indexes for "rent of shelter" and "services less rent of shelter." The differences between "shelter" and "rent of shelter" are miniscule. In terms of weight, the relative importance of "rent of shelter" was 31.3 percent in December 2012 and 20.3 percent in December 1982; in comparison, the relative importance for shelter was 31.7 percent in December 2012 and 21.3 percent in December 1982.

40 To compare changes in relative consumption between commodities and "services less OER," an experimental index must be constructed because there is no officially published index for "services less OER." This index can be constructed from the relative importance and price index data, with "rebasing" to account for expenditure weight updates. The percent price change for an index for "services less OER" from December 1982 to December 2012 can then be calculated, and expenditures in December 2012 based on pure price change can be obtained. Normalizing weights in both years then allows for a dissection of the relative price and quantity components.

41 See link in second bullet point at http://irrationalexuberance.com/. Moreover, U.S. Census Bureau data (see http://www.census.gov/const/uspriceann.pdf) show a 220-percent increase in median new home prices in the United States, from $69,300 in 1982 to $221,800 in 2010, compared with an increase of 126 percent in the annual average CPI-U U.S. City Average All Items index over the same period.

42 U.S. Census Bureau data at http://www.census.gov/const/C25Ann/sftotalmedavgsqft.pdf.

43 U.S. Census Bureau data at http://www.census.gov/housing/hvs/.

44 Because there is no officially published index for "services less other services," an experimental index had to be created for this category, in the same way as it was done for "services less OER."